Tadpole Books are published by Jump!, 5357 Penn Avenue South, Minneapolis, MN 55419, www.jumplibrary.com

Copyright ©2019 Jump. International copyright reserved in all countries. No part of this book may be reproduced in any form without written permission from the publisher.

Editor: Jenna Trnka **Designer:** Anna Peterson **Translator:** Annette Granat

Photo Credits: Michael Potter11/Shutterstock, cover; GroblerduPreez/iStock, 1; Alexey Osokin/Shutterstock, 2–3, 16tr; age fotostock/SuperStock, 4–5; Jurgen & Christine Sohns/Getty, 6–7, 16bl; Ralf Geithe/Shutterstock, 8–9, 16tl; Independent birds/Shutterstock, 10–11, 16bm; GoDog Photo/Shutterstock, 12–13, 16br; Exactostock-1598/SuperStock, 14–15, 16tm.

Library of Congress Cataloging-in-Publication Data
Names: Nilsen, Genevieve, author.
Title: Las crías del elefante / por Genevieve Nilsen.
Other titles: Elephant calves. Spanish
Description: Tadpole edition. | Minneapolis, MN: Jump!, Inc., (2019) | Series: Animales bebés de los safaris |
Audience: Age 3–6. | Includes index.
Identifiers: LCCN 2018037633 (print) | LCCN 2018038691 (ebook) | ISBN 9781641285421 (ebook) | ISBN 9781641285414 (hardcover : alk. paper) | ISBN 9781641286800 (pbk.)
Subjects: LCSH: Elephants—Infancy—Juvenile literature.
Classification: LCC QL737.P98 (ebook) | LCC QL737.P98 N5518 2019 (print) | DDC 599.6713/92—dc23
LC record available at https://lccn.loc.gov/2018037633

ANIMALES BEBÉS DE LOS SAFARIS

LAS CRÍAS DEL ELEFANTE

por Genevieve Nilsen

TABLA DE CONTENIDO

Las crías del elefante 2

Repaso de palabras 16

Índice 16

LAS CRÍAS DEL ELEFANTE

cría

Veo una cría de elefante.

¡Es un elefante bebé!

mamá

Sigue a mamá.

Mira sus orejas.

Mira su piel.

arrugas

Tiene arrugas.

Mira sus patas.

uña

Tienen uñas.

Mira su trompo.

trompo

¡Rocía!

Mira su boca.

Come.

REPASO DE PALABRAS

arrugas

boca

cría

orejas

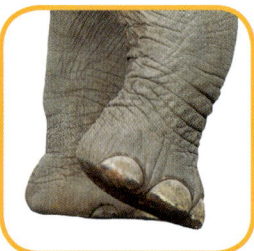
patas

trompo

ÍNDICE

boca 14
come 15
mamá 5
orejas 6

patas 10
piel 8
rocía 13
trompo 12